The Snake in the Cave

Part 4: The Sad Dragon

The focus in this book is on the split digraphs

'a-e, i-e, o-e' in the words:

flames   cave   came   snake   tape

safer   taken   outside   fire   bite

nose   drove   smoke   woke

The dragon looked sad. Wellington was not afraid of him. He asked him why he was sad.
'I have lost my flames,' said the dragon.

'I can only breathe out smoke. I have no fire. I cannot cook my sausages for my dinner. What will I eat?'

'Yap, yap, yap, yap!' Kevin and Lotty were barking at Wellington. He woke up. Oh! He was not in the cave. He was in his kennel.

The little dogs barked at Wellington until he went outside. On the path he saw a small black and green snake.

It was the snake that hissed at Kevin and Lotty.

It was not the snake that hissed at Wellington or tried to bite his nose.

Wellington sent Kevin and Lotty to fetch Farmer Robert. Farmer Robert looked at the snake. He thought it was a poisonous snake.

He told the dogs to stay and keep watch over the little snake while he hurried away to find some tools.

He came back with a garden fork and a brown box. He picked up the little snake with the fork and put it in the box.

He sealed the box with sticky tape. Then he put it in the back of his van and he drove the van away from the farm.

Robert took the snake to the vet in the town.

The vet put it in a glass tank until it could be taken to a safer place.

Vowel graphemes used in this book

ay, ai, a-e:	came place afraid flames cave snake away taken safer tape stay
ee, ea:	breathe eat green keep sealed
y, i-e, ie, i:	why my fire outside tried bite find while
o, o-e:	smoke woke nose over drove told
oo:	tools
oo:	took looked cook
ow, ou:	town brown out outside
or:	for fork or
er:	over safer dinner Robert Farmer
ar:	barking barked farmer garden farm
oi:	poisonous